Southern California Mountain Country
Places John Muir Walked and Places He Would Have Loved to Know

A Sierra Club Angeles Chapter Book

Photographs by Glenn Pascall
Graphic Design by Marjorie Alexander
Edited by George Watland & Mary Forgione

Printed in the United States of America

First Edition

ISBN 13: 978-0996119900
ISBN 10: 0996119906

John Muir photograph courtesy of the Library of Congress
"John Muir, seated, reading a book" 1912 - cph 3a10297

For more information and to order copies please visit
www.Angeles.SierraClub.org/Books

About this Book

Southern California Mountain Country was developed by the Sierra Club Angeles Chapter as part of the centennial marking the passing of John Muir in Los Angeles on December 24, 2014.

The Introduction to the book is based on a presentation made at "Remembering and Understanding John Muir," a Chapter-sponsored panel discussion held at Vroman's Bookstore in Pasadena in December 1, 2014.

The Muir readings and accompanying photographs were run in 82 daily installments on the Angeles Chapter's website beginning in October and concluding on December 24, 2014.

The purpose of this book is to honor the founder of the Sierra Club and to raise awareness of Southern California Mountain Country. The great majority of Muir quotes were inspired by his travels in the Sierra Nevada. Yet they fit the Southland high country – a much less celebrated region – remarkably well.

John Muir's eloquence and power of description are timeless. As with the treasures of nature, they are ours to "preserve, protect, enjoy."

Dedicated in appreciation
to John W. Robinson

Southern California's
mountain man extraordinaire

who has done so much
to make us realize
what is here

Mt. Baden-Powell and south-facing slopes of the
San Gabriel Mountains

*"The San Gabriel Mountains
are the most rigidly inaccessible range
I have ever encountered."*

*- John Muir, on climbs in the
Mt. Wilson region above Pasadena*

"The view from the summit of Mt. San Jacinto
Is the most magnificent in the world."

- John Muir, after his experience
as a member of the San Jacinto
Mountains survey of 1896

Looking south from atop San Jacinto

John Muir
April 21, 1838 - December 24, 1914

Introduction

-

Thanks to the warmth and power of his writing, and his practical impact on the conservation movement, the circle of those who appreciate and even love John Muir is large. Muir was a progressive who sounded great themes that made nature relevant to human experience in an era of cultural change.

First among these themes is that nature should be considered sacred in itself, whatever its source – whether from the deliberate intention of a supreme creative power or by the mysterious conjunction of astrophysical forces.

This crucial evolution in Muir's thought arose from his own life experience growing up in a severely strict religious household and then discovering the natural world on his own. In seeing the creation anew, he made nature accessible to people holding a vast range of beliefs.

Muir presented his message in lofty language - not surprising for one whose only permitted reading as a child was the Bible. The result is original thought expressed in classic eloquence.

Another of Muir's themes is wilderness as an aspect of nature. Muir celebrated wilderness. Today some believe the longing for wilderness must be replaced by an emphasis on nature in settings that are urban and accessible.

Close attention to Muir's writings reveals that his fascination was with nature itself, not with wilderness as a restrictive category. Muir's attention and imagination could be captured as fully by a leaf or a dewdrop as by a sweeping mountain panorama.

He raises our awareness, sensitivity and capacity for response as we encounter nature in the full range of settings, from the wilderness "vastation" of which Thoreau spoke to a dewdrop on a leaf in a vest pocket park in the heart of the city. Muir's message amplifies devotion to nature wherever we encounter it.

Did Muir's raptures arise in a lost age before today's resource exploitation and urban development? History tells a different story. California's modern era began with a massive act of disruptive resource extraction – the Gold Rush – in the heart of Muir's beloved Sierra Nevada.

In Muir's prime years, the corridor between the Bay Area and Yosemite pulsed with human activity. Much of it was not pretty – logging and use of Yosemite Valley for purposes hugely incompatible with its setting.

The simplest and clearest way to determine if Muir remains relevant is to ask where things would stand without him:

There would have been no visit by Teddy Roosevelt to Yosemite. None of the stunning eloquence from Teddy or Muir about the National Park System – America's best idea.

No founding of what is now a worldwide circle of friends of nature known as The Sierra Club, raising devotion for the planet from individual sentiment to sustained commitment. Far less chance that a host of other environmental organizations would have arisen from the Sierra Club model.

Without Muir, no redefinition of nature from God's handiwork to sacred in itself, and thus no invitation to people of all belief systems to join in the feast.

Without Muir, no supreme prophet speaking for justice toward nature as the prophets of old spoke for justice in human society. Yet at the end of the day, the point is not to see John Muir as a traditional religious figure but as a human being moved by the warmest glow of enthusiasm, asking us to share his joy as we encounter nature.

He had no doubt this deeper knowing would bring us to a place of greater devotion to nature. Thus the Sierra Club motto: Preserve, Protect, Enjoy.

What can we give back in response to his gift? We must strive to be the teachers of today and tomorrow, motivated as he was by a passion for the planet specific to our time yet relevant to all time.

In large part due to the inspired writings and tireless advocacy of John Muir, the Sierra Nevada of California is among the world's most celebrated ranges. By contrast, "The Southern Sierras of California," as Charles Francis Saunders called them, are virtually uncelebrated other than as a realm of mountain recreation conveniently located near a vast urban area.

In truth the Sierra Madre, as it was named before Saunders, holds a magnificent set of surprises and wonders that John Muir tasted yet never fully explored. The centennial of his passing in Los Angeles on Christmas Eve 1914 offers a welcome occasion to celebrate the time Muir spent in the Southland and to explore how remarkably well his writings about the Sierra Nevada serve as descriptions and depictions of secret places and secret moments in the Sierra Madre.

On some level, any adaptation of words from one experience to the reality of another place and time is suspect. The temptation must be resisted to take liberties that transpose the power of description and make assumptions of intention. Within the environmental movement, John Muir is too great a voice, too impactful a presence, for false attribution. Nothing other than the deepest respect and fidelity to the truths he taught will serve.

Yet those who know and love the Sierra Madre know that Muir would have loved it as well. Linking his passion for the Range of Light to that part of the world once poetically named the Lands of the Evening is not a falsification; rather it is a celebration of hidden connection.

In "John Muir: A Naturalist in Southern California," Elizabeth Pomeroy has given us the story of John Muir's connection to Southland. She writes that in June 1914, "just before his final illness, Muir appeared unexpectedly at a Sierra Club Campfire in Griffith Park… and left behind some vivid last memories of the naturalist and traveler…"

The centenary of that moment is an appropriate occasion to celebrate the essential connection between Muir and the region where the Sierra Club's first Chapter was formed – an event he openly celebrated in 1911 – and to more closely link the spirit of these magnificent yet neglected mountains with the spirit of Muir.

Barry Lopez perfectly summed up my part in this book when he said that the history and geography of any particular place "is recorded by those more or less committed by experience and inclination to that place."

John Muir perfectly summed up his part in this book when four decades before his death he wrote, "By his words a man may be said to walk the world long after he is in his grave."

The source for Muir quotations used here are twofold. "Gentle Wilderness: The Sierra Nevada" was published by Sierra Club Books in 1967 as part of its award-winning Format series. David Brower selected and edited Muir's words to accompany the photographs of Richard Kaufmann. The other source used here is "John Muir In His Own Words: A Book of Quotations" compiled and edited by Peter Browning and published by Great West Books in 1988.

Richard Kaufmann's sequence of Sierran images in "Gentle Wilderness" invite the viewer to "climb the mountain" from deep woods to snowy heights. This physical journey is framed on either side by context-setting reflections from Muir. Kaufmann's method is the inspiration for a similar sequence on these pages.

In the book before you, Muir's words are presented as lines of poetry. His natural cadence is poetic – an inborn gift that is inseparable from his power of utterance. What Muir said, combined with the ways he said it, make him an enduring voice.

Muir was an ecstatic celebrant of nature. Yet with the intuitive awareness of the artist he walked a tightrope between the effusive and the reflective. Thus he has not become dated by the sentiments and style of a cultural era that caused John Burroughs, Muir's friend and an observant naturalist, to lapse into relative obscurity.

Thanks to Muir's poetic gift, his passionate tributes when distilled to their essence are breathtakingly allusive and condensed. In the presentation here slightly over two thousand of his words serve to define more than eighty natural settings – a remarkably brief norm of twenty-four words per image.

Today every celebration of Earth as we have known it has the aspect of an elegy or even a eulogy. The Great Sierra and the Southern Sierra are equally vulnerable to heat and drought wrought by global climate change. The images recorded here invite the reader to experience these places. Yet the visual beauty of a flower, stream or snow bank has the haunting quality of a history that could become part of a past made no longer accessible by climatic events.

This book has multiple purposes: to honor the centennial of Muir's passing; to remember his presence over the decades in this part of the world; to apply the universal relevance of his words as a tool in exploring the mystery of nature; to suggest an equivalence between the two Sierras in their resonance of meaning for man; and to acknowledge our vulnerability to the irreversible disturbance of a delicate equilibrium.

Natural forces made both the Great Sierra and the Southern Sierras eloquent expressions of dynamic balance upon this Earth. That balance must be rendered sustainable, lest its loss be expressed in consequences even more severe for us than for Earth itself.

The Southern Sierras in their own way are as notable as the Great Sierra. These mountains rise as far from their base and display as stunning a range of contrast, as they shelter places of secret lushness from the relentless heat and dryness of a sun-soaked realm.

The most striking difference that emerges between the two Sierras is not – as one might expect – due to elevation and latitude. It is that the Southern Sierras have almost no gentle side, no gradual rise of terrain comparable to the western slope of the Sierra Nevada that Muir knew so well. Only Bear Valley in the San Bernardino Mountains offers more than a hint of the prevailing reality that defines much of the Great Sierra.

The Southern Sierras are constructed as if the precipitous eastern slope of the Sierra Nevada, where John Muir spent relatively little time, were matched by a western face that also plunged from the crest. There is also a contrast in geographic orientation. From Point Conception to San Gorgonio Pass, the backbone of the Southern Sierras runs not in a north-south axis but rises from the sea to the west and climbs steadily to the east. Thus this uplift is named the Transverse Ranges because it runs against the grain of American mountains.

At San Gorgonio Pass – a ten thousand foot gulf, deepest in the United States – the trend lines shift for reasons geologists have never fully explained. The San Jacinto Mountains, with the Santa Anas as modest echo, pivot to the south toward the tip of Baja California a thousand miles away, giving the fabled north face of San Jacinto the grip on a long sword that tapers toward Cabo San Lucas.

So it is that a relentlessly uncompromising aspect rather than lesser elevation or greater prevailing dryness sets the Southern Sierras apart from the Great Sierra. Here we discover sky islands perched atop knife-edge ridges that fall away from sheltered forests into abysses of chaparral and open deserts.

This improbable sweep of natural conditions complements the human drama of our region, which in its urban and commercial realm has given the world so many vivid myths of paradise in peril. Has nature perfectly played the role of backdrop to this paradox? Do our mountains define an alluring horizon, inspiring and enabling experiments that announce possibilities – and then reveal unexpected dimensions in startling ways?

If so, the Southern Sierra is of a piece with Southern California, extravagant in its boldness yet hinting of possible tragedy. It is well to recall that a century ago John Muir anticipated much that has brought us to this felt moment of peril upon the Earth. He disdained cities as corrupters of human character and he detested economically driven resource development as despoliation of natural treasure.

One of Muir's more elegantly restrained statements on these matters reads, "Compared to the intense purity and beauty and cordiality of nature, the most delicate refinements and cultures of civilization are gross barbarisms."

In this late hour some of us still seek to reconcile wilderness with cities – restless human enterprise with the self-generative works of nature. The challenge is to resolve a contradiction that Muir found unyielding, in order to achieve a synthesis he dismissed as unattainable. Since Roman times a gulf has persisted between societal dynamics and sustainable accommodation with the Earth as our host and independent reality. Evidence accumulates that the forces making this gulf unbridgeable are approaching critical mass.

As a magnificent landscape with strong wilderness aspects adjacent to a vast metropolis, there could be no better testing ground for the propositions in play than the Southern Sierras. In this grand game, Muir's soaring vision summons us to discover what can be salvaged, or better yet sustained, within these contending forces.

Muir was a visionary and thus in a certain sense an optimist. Muir was an idealist, and thus in a certain sense a pessimist in the face of surrounding evidence. Muir was a prophet and thus in a certain sense a voice of warning. Yet also Muir was a voice of inspiration, who with supreme eloquence celebrated the reward that might be ours if we act as stewards of the human future, which inescapably means being stewards of Earth.

We are his heirs. He has done much to make us conscious of who we are, what we are made of, and the choices are before us. Whatever may be the outcome that so clearly hangs in the balance, the words of John Muir carry ongoing relevance.

The Mountain Setting

Timber Mountain in the San Gabriel Mountains

Climb the mountains and get their glad tidings.
Nature's peace will flow into you
As sunshine flows into trees.
The winds will blow their freshness into you,
And the storms their energy,
While cares will drop off like autumn leaves.

God himself seems always to be doing his best here,
Working like a man in a glow of enthusiasm.

Topa Topa Bluff from Upper Ojai Valley in the
Ventura backcountry

Cucamonga Peak in the San Gabriel Mountains

In the midst of such beauty, pierced with its rays,
One's body is all one tingling palate.
Who wouldn't be a mountaineer!

Another glorious day
In which one seems to be dissolved and absorbed
And sent pulsing onward, we know not where.

Southern Santa Rosa Mountains from
Borrego Valley

Walk quietly in any direction
and taste the freedom of the mountaineer.

Mt. San Antonio (Old Baldy Peak) in the
San Gabriel Mountains

The Deep Woods

How beautiful a rock is made by leaf shadows.

Ponderosa and feldspar on Forsee Creek Ridge,
San Bernardino Mountains

When the leaves ripen in the fall
They become more beautiful than the flowers.

Wild Strawberry & Sugar Pine cones, Forsee Creek Ridge,
San Bernardino Mountains

Lichen-covered Granite, San Mateo Canyon,
Santa Ana Mountains

Rocky strength and permanence
Combined with the beauty of plants
Frail and fine and evanescent

Frostbitten fern above Horse Meadows,
San Bernardino Mountains

How soft and lovely the light
Streaming through this living ceiling
Revealing the arching branching ribs and veins
Of the fronds as the framework
Of countless panes of pale green and yellow plant-glass
Nicely fitted together, a fairyland
Created out of the commonest fernstuff.

Headwaters of the Santa Ana River, South Fork Meadows,
San Bernardino Mountains

A stream silently gliding,
Swirling, slipping, as if careful
Not to make the slightest noise.

Tiger lily in Cuyamaca Mountains,
San Diego backcountry

Nature is not so poor
As to possess only one of anything

I never saw a discontented tree.
They grip the ground as though they liked it,
And though fast-rooted
They travel about as far as we do.

Oak, pine and cedar on Palomar Mountain,
San Diego backcountry

The trees round about seem as perfect
In beauty and form as the lilies,
Their boughs whorled like lily leaves in exact order.

Aspen grove, Upper Fish Creek,
San Bernardino Mountains

Rose Valley Falls, Topa Topa Mountains,
Ventura backcountry

Drinking this champagne water is pure blessing
So is breathing the living air
Every movement of the limbs is pleasure
While the whole body seems to feel beauty
And feels homogeneous throughout,
Sound as a crystal.

In the ground, in the sky, spring work is going on.
New life, new beauty, unfolding, unrolling,
In glorious exuberant extravagance.

Lupine, cedar and pine, Mill Creek Canyon,
San Bernardino Mountains

From form to form, beauty to beauty,
Ever changing, never resting,
All are speeding on with love's enthusiasm
Singing with the stars
The eternal song of creation.

Ponderosa and dwarf willow below South Fork Meadows,
San Bernardino Mountains

Nature is ever at work building and pulling down,
Creating and destroying, keeping everything
Whirling and flowing, allowing no rest
But in rhythmical motion chasing everything
In endless song, out of one beautiful form
Into another.

Sycamore trunk, Caspers Wilderness Park,
Santa Ana Mountains

Black oak trees south of Idyllwild in the
San Jacinto Mountains

Beautiful and impressive contrasts meet you everywhere –
The colors of tree and flower, rock and sky,
Light and shade, strength and frailty,
Endurance and evanescence.

Pine forest and evening sky, Doane Valley, Palomar Mountain,
San Diego backcountry

The weather is pure gold,
White Cirrus flecks
And penciling around the horizon.

Pool, Icehouse Creek,
San Gabriel Mountains

For us there is no past, no future.
We live in the present and are full.

Every raincloud, however fleeting, leaves its mark
Not only on the trees and flowers whose pulses
Are quickened, but also on the rocks
Are its marks engraved
Whether we can see them or not.

Cedar trunk and granite boulders, Icehouse Creek,
San Gabriel Mountains

The death of flowers in a garden
Is only change from one form of beauty to another

Yucca skeleton, Icehouse Canyon,
San Gabriel Mountains

Live oak, Palomar Mountain,
San Diego backcountry

Some of the eternal beauty is always in sight,
Enough to keep every fiber of us tingling,
And this we are able to gloriously enjoy
Though the methods of its creation lie beyond our ken.

I gave heed to the confiding stream,
Mingled freely with the flowers and light,
And shared in the confidence of their exceeding peace

Columbine flowers, South Fork Meadows,
San Bernardino Mountains

Black oak and fir trees, Palomar Mountain,
San Diego backcountry

The level bottom seemed to be dressed like a garden –
Sunny meadows here and there
And groves of pine and oak.

Who could ever guess that so rough a wilderness
Should yet be so fine, so full of good things?

Lake Fulmor,
San Jacinto Mountains

This grand show is eternal.
It is always sunrise somewhere;
The dew is never dried all at once;
A shower is forever falling;
Vapor is ever rising.

Dawn at Humber Park looking toward Suicide Rock,
San Jacinto Mountains

Ponderosa pine and black oak trees, Barton Flat,
San Bernardino Mountains

The forests we so admired in summer
Seem still more beautiful and sublime
In this mellow autumn light.

The clearest way into the Universe
Is through a forest wilderness.

Pine, cedar and fir forest above Jenks Lake,
San Bernardino Mountains

The High Forest

Windblown ponderosa pine, Blue Ridge,
San Gabriel Mountains

Reading these great mountain manuscripts
Displayed through every vicissitude
Of heat and cold, calm and storm
We see that everything in Nature called destruction
Must be creation.

Nothing goes unrecorded.
Every word of leaf and snowflake and particle of dew,
As well as earthquake and avalanche,
Is written down in Nature's book.

Fir boughs, Mt. Abel, Ventura backcountry

*No portion of the world is so barren
As to not yield a precious harvest of divine truth.*

Manzanita skeletons, Tahquitz Peak,
San Jacinto Mountains

Life seems neither long nor short
And we take no more heed to save time or make haste
Than do the trees and stars.
This is true freedom.

Approaching storm, Devil's Slide,
San Jacinto Mountains

Stump and dwarf willow, Dawson Saddle,
San Gabriel Mountains

In the midst of these methodless ravings
I seek to spell out, by close inspection,
Things not well understood.
In the work of grave science I make but little progress
Yet these lawless wanderings will not be without value
As suggestive beginnings.

Western red cedar, Mt. Harwood,
San Gabriel Mountains

As we go on and on, studying this old life
In the light of the life beating warmly about us
We enrich and lengthen our own.

Black oak tree, Jenks Lake,
San Bernardino Mountains

Like trees in autumn shedding their leaves,
going to dust like beautiful days to night,
Proclaiming as with tongues of angels
The natural beauty of death.

San Antonio Falls, San Gabriel Mountains

Who could imagine beauty so fine in so savage a place?

2,000-year-old limber pine, Forsee Creek Ridge,
San Bernardino Mountains

A sturdy storm-enduring mountaineer of a tree,
Living on sunshine and snow,
maintaining tough health on this diet
For perhaps more than a thousand years.

Whitebark pine at 10,000 feet,
San Jacinto Mountains

How boundless the day seems
As we revel in these storm-beaten sky gardens
Amidst a congregation of onlooking mountains

The radiant host of trees stand hushed and thoughtful
Receiving the Sun's good-night,
As solemn and impressive a leave-taking
As if sun and trees were to meet no more.
The daylight fades, the color spell is broken
And the forest breaths free in the night breeze
Beneath the stars.

11,000-foot Jepson Peak towers over Christmas Tree
Slope at dusk in the San Bernardino Mountains

Root system of fallen limber pine, Forsee Creek Ridge,
San Bernardino Mountains

We rejoice and exult
In the imperishable wealth of the Universe
And faithfully watch and wait
The reappearance of everything
That melts and fades and dies about us.

Here it is six or seven thousand feet above the sea,
Yet in all that tranquil scene
We feel no remoteness,
No rest from care or chafing duties
Because here they have no existence.

Galena Peak from Mill Creek Canyon at dusk,
San Bernardino Mountains

The whole landscape shows design,
Like man's noblest sculptures.
How wonderful the power of its beauty!

Point Lookout across Santa Ana River Canyon,
San Bernardino Mountains

Fir tree shadows on spring snow, Upper Icehouse Canyon,
San Gabriel Mountains

Now, in the deep brooding silence
All seems motionless
As if the work of creation were done.
But in the midst of this outer steadfastness
We know there is incessant motion.

The snow is melting into music.

Cedar trunk and snowbank, Vivian Creek,
San Bernardino Mountains

The species of silver pine
Gives forth the finest music to the wind.
I think I could approximate
My position in the mountains
By this pine music alone.

Ice-bladed pine needles, Upper Icehouse Canyon,
San Gabriel Mountains

Through a meadow opening in the pine woods
I see snowy peaks…
How near they seem and how clear their outlines
On the blue air, or rather in the blue air,
For they seem to be saturated with it.

Ponderosa pine tree, Mt Waterman,
San Gabriel Mountains

The trees...
Seem unable to go a step further

Whitebark pine tree, Fuller Ridge,
San Jacinto Mountains

Of Snow & Rock

Primary life zones on Mt. San Jacinto,
from lower Sonoran to arctic-alipine

The sunshine is hot enough for palms, yet the snow
Round the arctic gardens at the summit is plainly visible
And between lie specimen zones
Of all the prime climates of the globe.

Ensemble above Banning,
San Jacinto Mountains

Patient observation and constant brooding
Above the rocks… is the way to arrive
At the truths that are graven
So lavishly upon them.

Tahquitz Rock from Humber Park, evening,
San Jacinto Mountains

Every rock in its walls seems to glow with life…
Awful in stern, immovable majesty,
How softly these rocks are adorned.

Sunrise, Mormon Rocks & San Gabriel Crest
from Cajon Junction, San Gabriel Mountains

Among these mighty cliffs and domes
There is no word of chaos;
Every word is elaborately and thoughtfully carved
As a crystal or shell.

The structure of the landscape
Is as striking in its main lines
As in its lavish richness of detail.

Gendarmes, Tahquitz Peak Ridge from above
Saddle Junction, San Jacinto Mountains

The rocks where exposure to storms is greatest
Are all the more lavishly clothed upon with beauty

Varicolored lichen on granite, Wellman Divide,
San Jacinto Mountains

Storm clouds forming over main crest from
Tahquitz Peak, San Jacinto Mountains

When I heard the storm I made haste to join it;
For in storms nature always has
Something extra fine to show us.

Tawny granite of Mt. San Bernardino, dark metamorphic rock
of Yucaipa Ridge, blue-distanced granite of Mt. San Jacinto
from Anderson Peak, San Bernardino Mountains

No longing for anything now or hereafter
As we go home to the mountain's heart.

We are now in the mountains and they are in us,
Making every nerve quiver, filling every pore and cell…
How glorious a conversion! In this newness of life
We seem to have been so always.

Mt. San Jacinto from 10,000 feet on San Gorgonio,
San Bernardino Mountains

Bathed in such beauty, watching the expressions
Ever varying on the faces of the mountains,
Would be endless pleasure.
And what glorious cloudlands, storms and calms –
A new heaven and a new earth every day.

Mt. San Antonio (Old Baldy Peak) from San Antonio Canyon,
San Gabriel Mountains

Looking north from Devil's Backbone, San Antonio Ridge,
San Gabriel Mountains

Great banks of snow and ice are pilled in hollows
On the cool precipitous north side.

Antsell Rock & Toro Peak from Tahquitz Peak,
San Jacinto & Santa Rosa Mountains

Drifting without human charts
Through light and dark, calm and storm,
I have come to so glorious an ocean.

Wherever you chance to be
Always seems at the moment
Of all places the best.

Alpenglow, Mt. San Bernardino from Mill Creek,
San Bernardino Mountains

Galena Peak & Yucaipa Ridge from Upper Vivian Creek,
San Bernardino Mountains

Oh, these vast, calm, measureless mountain days
In whose light everything seems equally divine.

Telegraph Peak & Jeffrey pine from Baldy Notch,
San Gabriel Mountains

I am only a piece of human mist
Drifting about these rocks and waters,
Heaven only knows how or wherefore.

Cucamonga Peak from San Antonio Canyon,
San Gabriel Mountains

Bathed in such beauty,
Watching expressions ever varying
On the faces of the mountains

As age comes on, one source of enjoyment after another
Is closed, but Nature's sources never fail.
Like a generous host, she offers here
Brimming cups in endless variety,
Served in a grand hall,
The sky its ceiling, the mountains its walls.

Mt. San Antonio & limber pine from Pine Mountain,
San Gabriel Mountains

Mt. San Antonio (Old Baldy Peak) at dusk, from Inspiration Point,
Blue Ridge, San Gabriel Mountains

Every day opens and closes like a flower,
Noiseless, effortless. Divine peace glows
On all the majestic landscape
In silent, enthusiastic joy

Nature's Gift

Pure water is poured from a hidden recess,
Schneider Creek, San Bernardino Mountains

No true invitation is ever declined.

One touch of nature
Makes the whole world kin.

Cedar trunk and bough, Icehouse Canyon,
San Gabriel Mountains

When we try to pick out anything by itself,
We find it hitched to everything else in the Universe.

Joshua trees and cloud streamers,
Little San Bernardino Mountains, Joshua Tree National Park

These beautiful days must enrich all my life.
They do not exist as mere pictures
But they saturate themselves into every part of my body
And live always

Mt. San Gorgonio, highest point in the Western hemisphere between
latitude 34 and 35 degrees north, San Bernardino Mountains

San Gabriel Crest, Mormon Rocks & container train
from Cajon Junction, San Gabriel Mountains

Nature is always lovely, invincible, glad,
Whatever is done or suffered by her creatures.
All scars she heals, whether in rocks
Or water or sky or hearts.

One is constantly reminded
Of the infinite lavishness and fertility of Nature –
Inexhaustible abundance and what seems enormous waste.
Yet when we look into any of her operations
That lie within reach of our minds,
We learn no particle of material is wasted or worn out.
It is eternally flowing from use to use,
Beauty to yet higher beauty.

Burl in bare ponderosa pine, Icehouse Saddle,
San Gabriel Mountains

Every soil-atom seems to yield
enthusiastic obedience to law –
boulders and mud-grains moving to music
as far-whirling planets

Metamorphic boulder, Icehouse Canyon,
San Gabriel Mountains

When one gains the blessings of one mountain day
Whatever his fate, long life, short life, stormy or calm,
He is rich forever.

Spur peak from Haugen-Lehman,
San Jacinto Mountains

Looking toward the Tehachapi Mountains from
California Poppy Reserve in Antelope Valley

There is in some minds a tendency
Toward wrong love
Of the marvelous and mysterious.
This leads to the belief that
Whatever is remote must be
Better than what is near.

Mt. San Gorgonio from Banning,
San Bernardino Mountains

The whole mountain
Appeared as one glorious manifestation of divine power,
Enthusiastic and benevolent, glowing like a countenance
With ineffable repose and beauty.

Mt. San Jacinto from Banning Bench,
San Jacinto Mountains

I used to envy the father of our race,
Dwelling as he did in contact with a new-made Eden
But I do so no more because I have discovered
That I also live in creation's dawn.

The morning stars still sing together
And the world, not yet half made,
Becomes more beautiful every day.

At such times one's whole body is an eye
And common skill and fortitude are replaced
By power beyond our call or knowledge.

Monolith, Lost Horse Valley, Little San Bernardino Mountains,
Joshua Tree National Park

Morning, cedar, pine and fir forest, above Jenks Lake,
San Bernardino Mountains

The woods are made for the wise and strong.
In their very essence they are counterparts of man.
All their forms and voices and scents seem,
As they really are, reminiscences
Of something already experienced.
Let a man see the grand woods for the first time
And he will enjoy their beauty and feel their fitness
As if he had learned of them from childhood.

San Gabriel Mountain sunset from Mill Creek Canyon,
San Bernardino Mountains

I only went out for a walk
And finally decided to stay out till sundown
For going out, I concluded,
Was really going in.

About the Photographs

The images in this book were taken over more than a half-century between 1961 and 2013 with a medium-format twin-lens camera and recorded on Ektachrome 120 film. A Tower camera with fixed 80 mm lens was used before 1970 and a Mamiya C220 camera since then with 55 mm, 80mm, 135 mm and 180 mm lenses.

The images in this book are as close to the actual scene as possible. The intent is that the reader might journey to each location and find it recognizable. Adjustments have been made only to compensate for the limitations of photographic paper versus film, with fidelity to nature the goal.

Most of these pictures were taken while hiking alone. The photographer's only regular companions were "Trails of the Angeles" and "San Bernardino Mountain Trails" by John W. Robinson. These thorough and trustworthy guides never misled and often opened up otherwise unknown possibilities.

About Glenn Pascall

The photographer, compiler of Muir quotes, and author of the Introductory essay on John Muir in Southern California Mountain Country is Sierra Club Angeles Chapter member Glenn Pascall.

As a photographer, Pascall's work has appeared at the Education Center of Joshua Tree National Park, the Gallery of the Art Institute of Colorado, Southern California hotel lobbies and Bay Area private collections. His images of regional wild country line the walls of the Sierra Club Angeles Chapter conference room in Los Angeles.

As a writer, Pascall's credits include "best columnist" awards from the American Society of Professional Journalists, and authoring a book that became the basis for a CBS News national television special.

Pascall serves as the Sierra Club Angeles Chapter librarian, Finance Chair, and head of the Chapter task force that oversees the shutdown of the region's only nuclear power plant.

Made in the USA
Charleston, SC
18 April 2015